INVESTIGATING LIGHT POLLUTION

LAURA PERDEW

Wonder Books
An Imprint of The Child's World®
childsworld.com

The Child's World
childsworld.com

Published by The Child's World®
800-599-READ • www.childsworld.com

Photography Credits
Photographs ©: Epic Stock Media/Shutterstock Images, cover, 2; Shutterstock Images, 5, 21, 31; iStockphoto, 6, 9, 24; Harry Collins Photography/Shutterstock Images, 10; Elena Berd/Shutterstock Images, 13; Charles T. Peden/Shutterstock Images, 14; Dima Berlin/Shutterstock Images, 17; Motortion Films/Shutterstock Images, 18; Evrim Ertik/iStockphoto, 22; Sander van der Werf/Shutterstock Images, 27; Red Line Editorial, 29

ISBN Information
9781503858084 (Reinforced Library Binding)
9781503860131 (Portable Document Format)
9781503861497 (Online Multi-user eBook)
9781503862852 (Electronic Publication)

LCCN 2021952369

Printed in the United States of America

BRINGING THE WORLD TO YOUNG READERS 1968

ABOUT THE AUTHOR

Laura Perdew is a mom, writing consultant, and author of more than 40 books for children. She lives and plays in Boulder, Colorado.

Too much light pollution can negatively affect ecosystems and people's health.

TABLE OF CONTENTS

CHAPTER ONE

WHAT IS LIGHT POLLUTION?

Even though it was late August, the evening was chilly. A light rain was falling. A family bundled up. They put on coats and orange vests. They grabbed flashlights and nets. As they walked through the quiet town, they swept their lights this way and that. They were on **puffin** patrol in Newfoundland and Labrador, Canada.

The youngest child pointed her light under a parked car. Underneath was a small baby puffin. The bird was lost and scared. Carefully, the girl dropped her net over it. She coaxed it out from under the car and put it in a plastic crate. The puffling was safe.

Puffins follow the light of the moon and stars to go to sea.

Puffins that lose their way to sea because of light pollution are in danger of being killed by cars or cats.

The puffling the family saved was one of the lucky ones. The young birds had just developed enough feathers to fly and leave their nests. Their nests were on a nearby island. The birds left at night to avoid predators. Normally, the moon and stars would guide the puffins out to sea. But it was cloudy that night, and the town's flickering lights confused the pufflings. They ended up on land by mistake.

A SHORT HISTORY OF ARTIFICIAL LIGHTS

For thousands of years, people used candles and oil lamps to light up their surroundings. The use of gas lamps grew in the 1800s. These lamps lit up cities in the United States and Europe. Then the electric light bulb was invented in the mid-1800s. Soon, electricity was available to more people. That made lighting simple and affordable. Because of this, the use of artificial lighting increased worldwide.

The family was part of the annual Puffin Patrol. Every year, hundreds of people volunteer to find and rescue puffins that lose their way to sea. Once the lost birds are found, they are taken to a safe place for the night. In the morning, all the rescued pufflings are taken to the beach to be released. Then they fly out to sea.

The **artificial** light that confuses pufflings is a growing problem around the world. The night sky is naturally very dark.

But in many places today, the sky glows at night because of artificial light. This is called light pollution. Most light comes from buildings and homes. Cars, streetlamps, and billboards are other sources of artificial light. Many places are so bright, the light can even be seen from space.

Some use of artificial lights is generally okay. It can make rooms feel safe and cozy. Electric light can also brighten people's way back home. But often there are too many lights. A lot of lights are too bright. Some lights do not cast light where they are supposed to. Others are not shielded. And many times, lights are not even needed at all. Plus, cities are getting bigger. Cities with more people use more electricity. As a result, light pollution is increasing. This causes problems for wildlife such as puffins. It is also harmful to plants and even to humans. But light pollution can be an easy problem to solve.

People who live in large cities are hardly able to see stars at night.

CHAPTER TWO

HARM TO WILDLIFE

All life on Earth depends on the cycle of day and night. However, light pollution has interrupted that natural cycle. Around the globe, nights have become too bright. This harms wildlife and plants that depend on this cycle for their survival.

Diurnal animals such as squirrels and songbirds rest at night. This is difficult in places with sky glow.

Owls are not able to hunt well when they are surrounded by artificial lights.

Sky glow is when the night sky becomes brighter because of light pollution. As a result, some animals do not get enough sleep.

Nocturnal animals rest during the day. They are active at night. Owls, foxes, and bats are nocturnal predators that use the darkness to sneak up on prey. With lights from human sources, hunting is more difficult. Also, it is harder for prey animals to hide from predators. Frogs and toads croak at night searching for a mate.

ADDED CARBON EMISSIONS

It takes electricity to turn on lights. Usually, coal, oil, and gas are burned to make electricity. This emits a lot of carbon dioxide into the air. Too much carbon dioxide in the air contributes to global warming. Global warming is responsible for stronger storms, melting ice caps, drought, heat waves, and more. All of this negatively impacts habitats, migration, and mating patterns of many species.

But because of light pollution, many frogs do not know when to croak. Some even stop mating in areas that are too bright. And if the frogs and toads do not reproduce, their populations decline.

Some animals use the dark night sky for navigation. Some birds, like puffins, depend on dark night skies. The artificial lights cause them to fly off course. Many hit buildings. Others **migrate** too early or too late because of the lights. Baby sea turtles also need dark skies. After they hatch, they need to go to the sea. The hatchlings use the moon to guide them. But if there are lights near the beach, they become confused. Some may head inland, toward the artificial lights. There, they are stranded, preyed upon, or hit by cars. Millions of baby sea turtles die every year because of this confusion caused by artificial lights.

Baby sea turtles are supposed to find their way to the sea. But artificial lights near the shore can confuse them.

White-lined sphinx moths are mainly nocturnal. They pollinate flowers at night.

Light pollution greatly affects insect populations, too. Many insects are attracted to light. Artificial light acts like a trap. Predators such as birds and bats can easily prey upon insects gathered around a light.

Light affects insects in other ways, too. Fireflies communicate with each other using their light signals. But too much artificial light makes it difficult to communicate. Dragonflies may lay their eggs in the wrong places because of light pollution. Usually, they lay their eggs in ponds or lakes. But the glow of a streetlamp can make other dark, shiny surfaces look like water. All of this has led to a decline in the insect population.

Everything is connected in nature. When one species is affected by light pollution, other species are affected. For example, nocturnal moths pollinate crops and plants. But because of light pollution, there are fewer moths to pollinate the crops and plants. Less pollination means that plants are not able to grow bigger fruit. It also means that plants cannot spread many seeds. The change in any species' population disrupts the function of other animal populations.

CHAPTER THREE

EFFECTS ON HUMANS

Light pollution does not affect only wildlife. Humans are also affected by too much artificial light. Today, 80 percent of the human population lives in a place with constant sky glow.

All living things have a natural, internal clock. This clock guides daytime and nighttime activity. Humans are diurnal. They are awake during the day and sleep at night. But too much light at night affects natural sleep patterns.

When it gets dark, human bodies produce melatonin. Melatonin is a natural chemical produced by the body at nighttime. This helps people fall asleep. It keeps the body healthy and helps other systems to function.

When people spend too much time on their phones at night, their sleep patterns can be affected.

Melatonin helps the cells in the body to repair themselves, too. But when there is too much light, the production of melatonin drops.

Lower levels of melatonin lead to health problems. Some people sleep poorly. Or they do not get enough sleep. Some are tired throughout the day. Other health problems include headaches, anxiety, and stress.

People's eyes can be permanently damaged if they are exposed to too much light.

And recent studies show a link between lower melatonin production and cancer. There is also increased risk of obesity, diabetes, and depression. The reason for these negative symptoms is that a human body is like a machine. When melatonin production is affected, a series of other chemical processes in the body are affected. That leads to a chemical imbalance.

HUMAN HISTORY WITH THE STARS

For thousands of years, humans have viewed the stars in the dark night sky. People saw pictures in the stars, like a giant dot-to-dot image. Some of these constellations are named after figures from myths, like Orion and Hercules. Some are named after animals, such as Aries (ram) and Taurus (bull). The stars were used to tell stories. They were used for navigation around the globe. Farmers also used stars to follow the seasons.

Light pollution affects people's eyes as well. The extra light can be overwhelming to parts of the eye. This can damage eyesight. The glare from artificial lights can affect vision, which may be uncomfortable. This causes some people to be unable to see when it is dark. Likewise, it is hard for the eye to adapt between bright light and no light. For drivers, that switch between light and dark can be dangerous.

People are spending a lot of money on lighting, too. When people use unnecessary light, money is wasted. More than 30 percent of outdoor lighting is not needed. Every year, $3 billion is spent on wasted light.

Another effect of light pollution is that night skies are not dark enough to see more than a few stars. Most people in the world will never see the Milky Way. Throughout history, looking at the stars in a dark night sky connected humans to the universe. This connection has been an inspiration for religion, science, art, and more. It allowed astronomers to learn and understand our universe. But today, most people are not able to gaze up at the beauty of a dark night sky.

BRIGHT CITIES FROM SPACE

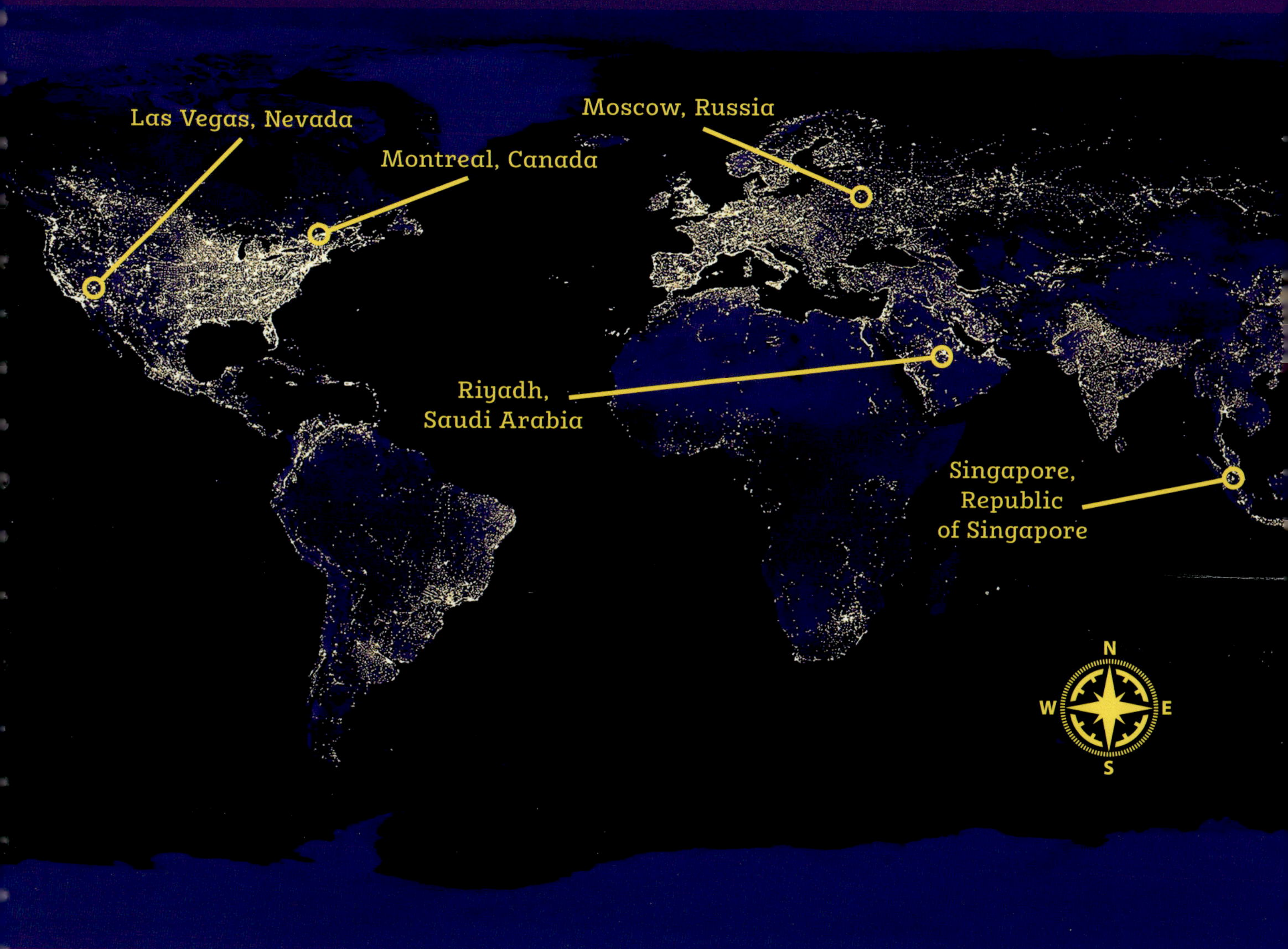

Major cities like Moscow, Riyadh, Montreal, and Singapore have the worst light pollution in the world. Las Vegas is known to be the brightest city on Earth from space.

CHAPTER FOUR

REDUCING LIGHT POLLUTION

Unlike other pollution problems, the solutions to light pollution are easy. One solution is to turn off the lights. That means city and building managers should turn off lights that are not needed. At home, indoor and outdoor lights not in use should be turned off.

Turning off a light when it is not needed can help lessen light pollution.

When using indoor lights, people can close their curtains. This keeps the light inside, so it does not spill out into the night.

Other devices that make light in the home should be off at night for human health. This includes nightlights, televisions, phones, and other electronic devices. Turning off these devices will help people get better sleep and stay healthy.

Another solution to light pollution is to make changes to existing lighting inside and out. Lights should be fully shielded on the top and sides. This directs the light downward. Light will not escape sideways or into the sky, which creates sky glow. All lights should be no brighter than necessary. Lights should be on only when needed. Outdoor lighting can be connected to motion sensors. Then the lights will turn on only when there is movement in an area.

Outdoor lights that point downward can help reduce light pollution.

The color of light is important. LED lights are popular because they save electricity and money. Most LED bulbs are a mix of blue, green, and red light. They have a high **color temperature**. That means the light looks brighter and has cooler tones. However, blue and violet light strain people's eyes more than other colors. They are also the most polluting. Blue and violet light scatter more and have a greater reach than other colors.

This contributes to sky glow. Light bulbs that are amber or yellow are the best choice for indoor and outdoor lights. Warm-white or filtered bulbs are also a good choice. These bulbs have lower color temperature compared to blue light. The light is less harsh.

Reducing excess artificial light is especially important during bird migrations. All year, birds are impacted by artificial lights. But during migration periods, more birds are on the move. Every year, millions of migrating birds in North America die because of light pollution. Some are killed when they collide with buildings. Others die of exhaustion as they fly around confused. Organizations are working to raise awareness to protect birds. For example, a partnership of groups in Philadelphia, Pennsylvania, created Bird Safe Philly. The program was started after thousands of migrating birds in 2020 collided with buildings in the city and died.

Bird Safe Philly now works to reduce light pollution to protect migrating birds. During key migration times, people in the city are encouraged to dim or turn off lights at night. There are similar efforts around the country.

Governments are helping, too. New lighting laws and limits are going into effect around the world. Slovenia passed a law in 2007. Now all outdoor lighting must be shaded. Also, the lights must not be brighter than a certain level. France passed a similar law in 2019. In only two years, France saw light pollution decrease by 6 percent. And in the United States, 17 states have light pollution laws.

The International Dark Sky Association is a **conservation** program. Since 1988, it has worked to raise awareness and preserve dark skies. It supports responsible lighting policies in places like cities and parks. It educates the public, too. And it recognizes places that have reduced light pollution.

In 2001, Flagstaff, Arizona, became the first International Dark Sky Place. The city has modified its outdoor lighting. Its streetlights have light bulbs that pollute less. They are shielded. And many are on timers.

Flagstaff is a role model for cities, businesses, and homes to protect dark night skies. Light pollution has simple solutions. Everyone can take part. Everyone can help spread the word. And everyone can turn off a light!

When people do their part in reducing light pollution, night skies can become more visible.

FAST FACTS

- Because of light pollution, the night skies are no longer dark in many places around the world.
- Light pollution disrupts the natural cycle of day and night.
- Sky glow at night harms wildlife, habitats, and humans.
- Animals need the dark night sky for navigating, breeding, hunting, and hiding from predators.
- Light pollution affects sleep patterns in humans. This can lead to anxiety, depression, and disease.
- Light pollution can strain and damage people's eyesight.
- Due to light pollution, many people in the world cannot see the Milky Way or more than a few stars.
- The solution to light pollution is simple. People can use dimmer lights, shielded lights, and amber-colored bulbs.
- Many cities and organizations around the world are working to raise awareness about light pollution to protect dark night skies.

UNDERSTANDING LIGHT POLLUTION

MATERIALS

- A flashlight
- Dark construction paper
- A sharp pen, pencil, or pin
- A dark room

DIRECTIONS

1. Using a sharp pen, pencil, or pin, poke a few holes through a piece of dark construction paper. Create your own pattern with the holes.
2. In a completely dark room, put your construction paper over a flashlight. Shine the flashlight on the wall or ceiling to see your pattern.
3. Next, increase the amount of light in the room. This might be done by turning on a dim light or opening a curtain slightly. Look at your pattern again. Can you still see it?
4. Increase the amount of light in the room again and look at the pattern. Is it getting harder to see?

GLOSSARY

artificial (ar-ti-FISH-ul) Something that is artificial is man-made and not natural. Artificial light can be harmful to migrating birds.

color temperature (KUHL-ur TEM-pur-uh-chur) Color temperature describes the type of light provided by a light bulb. Blue light has a much higher color temperature than yellow light.

conservation (kon-sur-VAY-shuhn) Conservation protects forests, wildlife, and natural resources. Many conservation programs are working to reduce light pollution.

diurnal (dy-UR-nul) Diurnal describes animals that are active during the day. Diurnal animals include humans, dogs, and elephants.

migrate (MYE-grate) Migrate means to move from one area to another when seasons change. Some birds migrate to warmer places in the winter.

nocturnal (nok-TUR-nuhl) Nocturnal animals are active during the night and sleep during the day. Nocturnal predators need darkness to hunt at night.

puffin (PUF-in) A puffin is a seabird living in northern and Arctic regions. Puffin movements may be impacted by light pollution.

WAYS YOU CAN HELP

- Turn off all lights that are not needed, especially at night.
- Before going to bed, put away your smartphone or laptop.
- Spread the word about how light pollution affects wildlife, habitats, and people.
- Write to a local politician or government official if your neighborhood has streetlamps that are too bright or are not shielded.

FIND OUT MORE

In the Library

Ganeri, Anita. *Star Stories: Constellation Tales from Around the World*. Philadelphia, PA: Running Press Kids, 2019.

Ganeri, Anita. *Through the Night Sky*. New York, NY: DK Publishing, 2020.

Unwin, Mike. *Migration*. New York, NY: Bloomsbury, 2019.

On the Web

Visit our website for links about investigating light pollution: **childsworld.com/links**

Note to Parents, Teachers, and Librarians: We routinely verify our Web links to make sure they are safe and active sites. So encourage your readers to check them out!

INDEX